100

THINGS TO DO IN
LITTLE ROCK
BEFORE YOU
DIE

Thanks for all you do to promote Little Rock!

100

2nd Edition

THINGS TO DO IN
LITTLE ROCK
BEFORE YOU
DIE

CELIA ANDERSON AND GRETCHEN HALL

REEDY PRESS

Library of Congress Control Number: 2018936112

ISBN: 9781681061443

Design by Jill Halpin

Cover photo courtesy of the Little Rock Convention & Visitors Bureau.

Printed in the United States of America
18 19 20 21 22   5 4 3 2 1

Please note that websites, phone numbers, addresses, and company names are subject to change or cancellation. We did our best to relay the most accurate information available, but due to circumstances beyond our control, please do not hold us liable for misinformation. When exploring new destinations, please do your homework before you go.

DEDICATION

To our mothers, Dorothy Hall and Sarah Hinton, for bestowing leadership skills and teaching us perseverance, independence, and work ethic. For teaching us to not just *lean in*, but to support and encourage others along the way. Words cannot adequately express the sincere appreciation and admiration we have for each of you!

And to KK, Debbie, Gabby, Gwinn, and Rece, the next generation, and whose character and integrity at a young age give us hope for the future.

● ●

CONTENTS

• •

• •

Music and Entertainment

Sports and Recreation

● ●

Culture and History

• •

• •

• •

INTRODUCTION

Welcome to Little Rock, Arkansas's capital city and our hometown! Most people know we are home to the Clinton Presidential Center and Little Rock Central High, but did you know that we are also home to an amazing twenty-plus-mile river trail and the Big Dam Bridge—the longest bicycle/pedestrian bridge in the country? What about the fact that we are also home to the oldest state capitol west of the Mississippi River? Yep, it's now a great museum—the Old State House. The Arkansas Travelers is one of the nation's longest running minor league franchises. Little Rock is home to the Esse Purse Museum, the only one in the United States, and one of three in the world. We are also the only place in the world to boast two floating Naval vessels that bookend World War II, the USS *Razorback*, the longest-serving submarine in the world, and the tugboat *Hoga*. The Little Rock Air Force Base is the largest training and maintenance facility for C-130 aircraft.

We hope you come hungry! Many say cheese dip was invented in Arkansas and our Little Rock chefs have mastered the decadent flavors of melted greatness. But that's not all, the culinary delights are endless. We may have the most locally owned restaurants of any city our size. From artisan brews, to handmade chocolates and ice cream, to amazingly creative meals, this book only begins to scratch the surface. We could name more than one hundred great places to dine, so for a complete list of Little Rock restaurants check out DineLR.com. *Forbes Travel Guide* realized the city's culinary charm, naming Little Rock one of its "Five Secret Foodie Cities."

What we love most about our city is the people and unique neighborhoods. Yes, we are Arkansas's largest city and offer lots of big-city amenities, but we have a heart for hometown. Southern hospitality is the real thing here. Take time to explore our neighborhoods, each with its own unique style, amenities, and fun-loving people.

In recent years, Little Rock has undergone a tremendous renewal. A catalyst for the city's success has been the Clinton Presidential Center, propelling this region as a true tourist destination. And, the recently renovated historic Robinson Center is the city's state-of-the-art performance hall and anchor to the downtown convention, arts, and entertainment district. Wonderful attractions, award-winning restaurants, entertainment venues, and new hotels await you.

There's never been a better time to visit Little Rock. We know that while here you will discover why we say, "Life is Better with a Southern Accent." Of course there are more than one hundred things to do in Little Rock, but this book will get you started on your journey to experiencing the magic of the capital city and you just might have to extend your stay.

• •

ACKNOWLEDGMENTS

Our first acknowledgment is to recognize faith, family, and friends that have provided encouragement and support throughout the years. To the wonderful community and public and private leadership that work each day to make our city a better place for its citizens and visitors.

Reedy Press, you have been amazing. Thank you for choosing us to share our city with the world. Life is indeed better with a southern accent! To all the local business owners who help make Little Rock an astonishing city, we are grateful for your hard work and passion for our city.

FOOD AND DRINK

DRINK LIKE A LOCAL
WITH LOCALLY LABELED

In Little Rock we like to keep things local, even our alcohol. With numerous homegrown craft breweries, wineries, and a distillery, we have a drink for everyone. Locally Labeled is your passport to the local beverage scene. The concept is simple: first you visit the Locally Labeled website below, then download the passport, visit participating locations, and get customized stickers to win a Locally Labeled t-shirt or coaster! Locally Labeled is a must do for anyone visiting the city. You will experience Arkansas's first legal distillery since prohibition, Rock Town Distillery, founded by Phil Brandon in 2010. Here you can find a Hot Doctor and Apple Pie, both over ice and in a glass! Then there is Diamond Bear Brewing Co., where they make their famous Strawberry Blonde beer. Whether your drink of choice is beer, wine, or whiskey, Little Rock has a spot for you!

Locally Labeled
littlerock.com/food-drink/locally-labeled-beverages

TIP
Don't want to drive? No problem, find twenty-three friends and take the Toddy Trolley!
toddytrolley.com, 501-603-0113
Or take a tour tasting with Arkansas Brews Cruise
arkansasbrewscruise.com, 501-410-6078

Locally Labeled Participants

Blue Canoe Brew Co.
425 E. 3rd St., Little Rock
501-492-9378
bluecanoebrewco.com

Core Public House
411 N. Main St.
North Little Rock, 501-372-1390
1214 S. Main St. Little Rock
501-353-2489
corebeer.com

Damgoode Pies Brewpub
500 President Clinton Ave.
Little Rock
501-353-1724
damgoodepies.com

Diamond Bear Brewing Co.
600 N. Broadway St.
North Little Rock
501-708-2729
diamondbear.com

Flyway Brewing Company
314 N. Maple St.
North Little Rock
501-812-3192
flywaybrewing.com

Lost Forty Brewing
501 Byrd St., Little Rock
501-319-7275
lost40brewing.com

Rebel Kettle Brewing
822 E. 6th St., Little Rock
501-374-2791
rebelkettle.com

Refined Ale Brewery
2221 S. Cedar St., Little Rock
501-663-9901

Stone's Throw Brewing
402 E. 9th St., Little Rock
501-244-9154
stonesthrowbeer.com

Vino's Brewpub
923 W. 7th St.
Little Rock, 501-375-8466
vinosbrewpub.com

**An Enchanting
Evening Winery**
29300 AR-300, Roland
501-330-2182
anenchantingevening.com

**River Bottom Winery at
BoBrook Farms**
13810 Combee Ln., Roland
501-868-8860, 501-519-5666
bobrookfarms.com

**Water Buffalo & Buffalo
Brewing Co.**
106 S. Rodney Parham Rd.
Little Rock, 501-725-5296
thewaterbuffalo.com

Rock Town Distillery
1201 Main St., Little Rock
501-280-0556
rocktowndistillery.com

START
AT THE BEGINNING AT FRANKE'S

What better place to start your Little Rock food journey, than at the beginning? That's right, Franke's Cafeteria is Arkansas's oldest restaurant. Dating back to 1919, this family-owned business has survived in Arkansas for nearly a century. The original vision of C.A. Franke was a doughnut shop opened in 1919, and by 1924 Franke's Cafeteria was born. W.J. Franke was the second generation to run the cafeteria before passing it on to third generation W.K. "Bill" Franke in 1983. Today Bill and his wife Carolyn still run the business. Franke's now has three locations in Little Rock, all serving up award-winning southern home cooking. Visit Franke's, where you are certain to feel at home, and don't skip the egg custard pie!

Franke's Market Place
Market Place Shopping Center
11121 N. Rodney Parham Rd., Little Rock
501-225-4487, frankescafeteria.com

Franke's Downtown
Regions Center Building
400 Broadway St., Little Rock
501-372-1919

"Sack It" by Franke's
Regions Center Building
400 Broadway St., Little Rock
501-372-4177

EAT LIKE A PRESIDENT
AT DOE'S EAT PLACE

Looking for a dive with food that tastes like your mother's? Doe's Eat Place is the place to be. You won't find fancy tablecloths or waiters and waitresses dressed in their Sunday best, but you will find steaks that put any world-class steakhouse to shame. It all began when George Eldridge grew tired of flying friends and clients to Doe's Eat Place in Greenville, Mississippi, where he found the best tamales and steaks around. Soon he contracted the right to bring both the name and menu to Little Rock. Not only did it save him a lot of gas, it quickly became a local favorite. Doe's most famous regular is none other than former President Bill Clinton. In 1992, when then-candidate Clinton was interviewed by *Rolling Stone* magazine, the backdrop was Doe's Eat Place.

1023 W. Markham St., Little Rock
501-376-1195
doeseatplace.net

ENJOY UPSCALE CUISINE
AT THE CAPITAL HOTEL

There is no place in Little Rock like the Capital Hotel. The boutique property has been the very definition of class in the city for over thirty years. Aside from offering a unique hotel experience, the Capital Hotel also serves up exquisite cuisine. They have two restaurants on property, One Eleven at the Capital and the Capital Bar and Grill. One Eleven at the Capital is the total dining experience complete with upscale cuisine, excellent service, and a very inviting atmosphere. There you can enjoy the food of James Beard Award-winning Chef Joel Antunes. The Capital Bar and Grill is where you go for drinks and comfort food. The popular bar is perfect for after-work cocktails and catching some jazz from the Ted Ludwig Trio who play there every Thursday through Saturday.

111 W. Markham St., Little Rock
501-374-7474
capitalhotel.com

TIP
The Capital Hotel is famous for their spiced pecans and pimento cheese.
Try them both.

DISCOVER WHERE TRADITION MEETS INNOVATION
AT TRIO'S

The tag line on their logo says it all, "Where tradition and innovation come to dine." Trio's has been a Little Rock staple for more than thirty-two years. A few mainstays on the menu include the Peck Special Salad, shrimp enchiladas, and the Voodoo Pasta, but the best thing about Trio's is their use of locally sourced ingredients. Their menu changes often to highlight in-season produce from local growers. Their bar menu also offers tasty seasonal selections. Moreover, do not miss their Sunday brunch; it's one of the best in town!

8201 Cantrell Rd., Ste. 100, Little Rock
501-221-3330
triosrestaurant.com

FIND A FLAVORFUL HISTORY
AT PETIT & KEET

New to Little Rock's restaurant scene but entrenched in our city's culinary history, Petit & Keet hit the mark. They refer to the restaurant as "culinary-driven, polished casual." The culinary history is in the names that adorn the building, Jim Keet and Louis Petit, the partners in the new venture. Keet's roots in Arkansas began in 1975 when he moved here to open the first Wendy's franchise. Since then, he and his family have created numerous restaurant concepts, including Taziki's Mediterranean Café and Paninis and Company. As for the Belgium native, Petit also came to Little Rock in 1975 to be part of the fine-dining restaurant Jacques and Suzanne. So many great Little Rock chefs trained under Petit; his lineage within Little Rock cuisine is unmatched. Together the combo is creating a true taste of the city's culinary history.

1620 Market St., Little Rock
501-319-7675
petitandkeet.com

Looking for beef?
Try these local favorite burger joints!

David's Burgers
3510 Landers Rd., North Little Rock
501-353-0387

101 South Bowman Rd., Little Rock
501-227-8333
davidsburgers.com

Ottenheimer Market Hall
400 President Clinton Ave., Little Rock

Monkey Burger
4424 Frazier Pike, Little Rock
501-490-2222

Big Orange
207 N. University Ave., Ste. 100, Little Rock
501-379-8715
bigorangeburger.com

17809 Chenal Pkwy., Ste. G-101, Little Rock
501-821-1515

The Box
1023 W. 7th St., Little Rock
501-372-8735

Buffalo Grill
1611 Rebsamen Park Rd., Little Rock
501-296-9535

CREATE A MEMORY
AT CACHE

In the heart of downtown Little Rock, Cache has quickly become a local favorite. The city can thank Rush and Payne Harding for their vision of culinary greatness. The father-son duo wanted to bring a contemporary dining experience to downtown, one that fostered the spirit of togetherness. It is not uncommon for business men and women to find themselves at Cache winding down from the busy work day. The upstairs bar and balcony that overlooks President Clinton Avenue offers a place to relax, enjoy signature cocktails, and listen to live music. Cache also offers a banquet room for private events and has become a go-to for corporate meetings and events. Dining at Cache will be an experience that you won't soon forget. What's with the name? The iconic Cache River located in Arkansas's Delta is where Rush was born and raised, and there is a nod to the dictionary definition of a "cache" which is a place for storing valuable possessions. What are you waiting for? Create a memory at Cache!

425 President Clinton Ave., Little Rock
501-850-0265
cachelittlerock.com

DINE WITH THE BEST
AT SONNY WILLIAMS' STEAK ROOM

Be sure to dress to impress and make a reservation if you plan on going to Sonny Williams'. Thrillist.com named the downtown steak room Arkansas's best steakhouse. Since Little Rock is home to many, this is no small feat! Located in the River Market District downtown, Sonny Williams' opened in Little Rock in 1999. Since then they have served a steak that is both aged and tender. Pair it with a wine from an extensive wine list and delicious sides of your choice. For non-beef eaters, the finest pork, lamb, chicken, and seafood are also on the menu. With complimentary valet and stellar service, Sonny Williams' has overlooked no detail. Did we mention they also have a piano bar?

500 President Clinton Ave., Ste. 100, Little Rock
501-324-2999
sonnywilliamssteakroom.com

TIP
Not ready to call it a night after dinner? Take a stroll through the Vogel Schwartz Sculpture Garden in Riverfront Park. It has an amazing collection of public art.

CELEBRATE SOUTHERN CULTURE
AT SOUTH ON MAIN

Chef Matthew Bell is one of Little Rock's most creative chefs, with a unique flair for culinary cuisine. The lunch menu at South on Main includes daily blue plate specials ranging from classic fried chicken and mac and cheese to melt-in-your-mouth barbecue brisket tacos. If you can wait until dinner, you can have Duck Breast with Nellie Mae's Cornbread Dressing, Granny Beans & Giblet Gravy. There are also mouthwatering vegetarian options, such as the Hoppin' John Veggie Burger. While you are dining, you can also enjoy programming directly from *Oxford American* magazine, including film screenings and musical performances. South on Main is more than a restaurant, it's a community movement, the heartbeat of SoMa, Little Rock's South Main Neighborhood.

1304 Main St., Little Rock
501-244-9600
southonmain.com

TIP
The restaurant is across the street from The Bernice Garden.
Take a few extra moments to visit the garden.
The sculptures alone are a sight to be seen.

SAVOR THE RAMEN
AT ARKANSAS HEART HOSPITAL

We know, we know, you probably think we are crazy for suggesting hospital food as a culinary delight, but just hear me out. The chef at Arkansas Heart Hospital is making a name for himself, and the hospital has become a true ramen destination. It has even been featured on CBS News. The hospital's CEO, Bruce Murphy, wanted to serve food that people would want to eat, with a focus on fresh and delicious, and oh yeah, Japanese ramen had to be part of the menu. Why? Because he liked it. So much so, he sent Chef Coby Smith to Tokyo to learn how to cook ramen. We would say the venture has been a success. Three days a week, the line wraps around the lobby as people come from across the city to enjoy a ramen lunch. Get there early, as some days it is hard to find parking in the hospital lot, but great news, this delicious lunch won't break the bank!

1701 S. Shackleford Rd., Little Rock
arheart.com/culinary

SUPPORT LOCAL FARMERS
AT THE ROOT CAFE

Since 2008, The Root has been an avid supporter of Arkansas farmers. Their mission is to build community through local food. Because of this, they have become much more than a restaurant. Located in the heart of the South Main (SoMa) neighborhood, The Root has lived up to its name by creating a sound foundation on which the community can grow. Aside from great food, they offer several different activities from workshops to beard-growing contests! It is not uncommon to see people sitting along the sidewalk dining area conversing about environmental issues. The Root Cafe is a favorite among clean eaters. A few of the farmers they support include Apple Jack Farm in North Little Rock, Armstead Mountain Farm in Jerusalem, Little Rock Urban Farming in Little Rock, and Pulaski Heights Elementary Garden in Little Rock.

1500 Main St., Little Rock
501-414-0423
therootcafe.com

TASTE BRAZILIAN CUISINE
AT CAFÉ BOSSA NOVA

Thanks to native Brazilian Rosalia Monroe and her family for bringing Brazil to Little Rock. Enjoy authentic Brazilian food in a culturally astute atmosphere. Menu items include starters like Pão de Queijo, a Brazilian-style cheese bread made with gluten free yucca root flour, milk, eggs, and cheese. Or try a main course such as Panquecas de Frango, Brazilian chicken crepes baked in Catupiry cheese sauce, or homemade marinara sauce served over rice and a Mista salad. As you can see, there is nothing American about Bossa Nova. For dessert, you can slide next door to Rosalia's Bakery for more traditional treats. Oh, don't forget Sunday brunch from 10:30 a.m. to 2 p.m., where you can enjoy live music and cuisine. But get there early, it's a local after-church favorite.

2701 Kavanaugh Blvd., Little Rock
501-614-6682
cafebossanova.com

BE BRAVE. BE NEW.
AT BRAVE NEW RESTAURANT

The awards for this restaurant go on and on. From best romantic restaurant to best chef to best business lunch, Brave New Restaurant has won them all. Service here is second to none. The staff is friendly and knowledgeable and the food is impeccable. Situated on the Arkansas River, you can choose to dine inside or outside for a scenic view. Either way, it will be money well spent. When driving there, be careful not to miss it. It is on the second floor of an office building, so you have to take the elevator up. Once you get there the ride will have been worth it. Offering a classy atmosphere, with oil lamp candles on the tables and a menu with something for everyone, Brave New has taken its spot among the restaurant elite. Going for lunch? May we recommend the Nontraditional Grilled Cheese? Trust me on this one.

2300 Cottondale Ln., Ste. 105, Little Rock
501-663-2677
bravenewrestaurant.com

LOVE THE FOOD
AT CAFE PREGO

Three words describe this restaurant: great Italian food. Prego takes pride in every dish on their one-page menu. This is not your typical stuffy place with wait staff running around in neckties. No, Prego is down-home Italian. The small locally-owned place has no interest in keeping up with the Jones's, only serving immaculate entrées. This they do very well. The focaccia bread is always a great start. Many recommend the Tortellini Carbonara; it has quite the reputation around town. If you are the type of diner who does not need bells and whistles, Prego is the place for you. The charming establishment has only one thing in mind, serving up good food. If weather permits, ask to sit on the patio. You'll be glad you did.

5510 Kavanaugh Blvd., Little Rock
501-663-5355

GRATIFY YOUR SWEET TOOTH
AT LOBLOLLY CREAMERY

Specializing in small batch ice cream, fizzy sodas, and other sweet treats, Loblolly Creamery builds every recipe from the ground up, using fresh, seasonal ingredients, without the use of any premixes, preservatives, colorings, and artificial stabilizers. At their Scoop Shop, you will find everything made from scratch, such as house-made gluten-free cones, seasonal handcrafted sodas, buttercream macaroons, milkshakes, and decadent ice cream sandwiches. They also love partnering with local farms, breweries, and food crafters, and give back to the community by partnering with local nonprofits. Several Little Rock restaurants serve their ice cream, so keep an eye out for it on the menu. They also have a sweet food truck that is a regular at local events and festivals.

1423 S. Main St., Little Rock
501-503-5164
loblollycreamery.com

What are pastries without coffee?
Try these local coffee shops

Mylo Coffee
2715 Kavanaugh Blvd., Little Rock
501-747-1880, mylocoffee.com

Nexus Coffee & Creative
301B President Clinton Ave., Little Rock
501-295-7515, nexuscoffeear.com

Guillermo's Gourmet Coffee
10700 N. Rodney Parham Rd., Suite A2, Little Rock
501-228-4448

The Meteor Café
1001 Kavanaugh Blvd., Little Rock
501-664-7765, themeteorcafe.com

River City Coffee
2913 Kavanaugh Blvd., Little Rock
501-661-1496, rivercitycoffeelr.com

Zeteo Coffee
610 President Clinton Ave., Little Rock
501-386-3227, zeteocoffee.com

Mugs Cafe
515 Main St., North Little Rock
501-379-9109, mugscafe.org

Andina Cafe
433 E. 3rd St., Little Rock
501-376-2326, andina-cafe.com

Blue Sail Coffee Co.
417 Main St., Little Rock
501-733-8006, bluesail.coffee

DON'T DANCE
AT SAMANTHA'S TAP ROOM
AND WOOD GRILL

At first glance you may mistake this for a dance studio, but please do not be confused. There is no tap dancing around anything at Samantha's Tap Room, they are straight upscale and comfortable with astounding fare. Located in one of Little Rock's newest neighorhoods, The Main Street Creative Corridor, Samantha's has been instrumental in breathing life back into Main Street. Offering their entire beer and wine list on tap (thirty-two beers and twenty wines) makes them not only a popular spot, but also the only restaurant in Arkansas to do so. Winner of the 2015 Free Flow Wine Keggy People's Choice Award, Samantha's has received national recognition, and rightfully so. The menu selection is just as broad as the wine and beer list, and it's all cooked by way of wood fire.

322 Main St., Little Rock
501-379-8019
samstap.com

STUFF YOURSELF
AT FLYING FISH

No, the fish do not fly, but they do fry and they never disappoint! Flying Fish is "fast-casual"-style dining. You line up, order, pick your seat, and wait for your number to be called. While you wait, enjoy fresh hushpuppies and coleslaw, but save room for your entrée. If you like East Texas fish joints, you will love Flying Fish. Here you can get shrimp, oysters, crab legs, and crawfish in season. There is also a special selection of trout, grilled salmon, or tilapia presented daily. For the non-seafood-lovers, they have fresh salads, hamburgers, and chicken tenders. The best thing is, Flying Fish is open seven days a week from 11 a.m. to 10 p.m. So whatever time you ride into town, stop at Flying Fish. You will be glad you did. And if you like a little kick ask them to "make it snappy!"

511 President Clinton Ave., Little Rock
501-375-3474
flyingfishinthe.net

SOAK YOUR BREAD
AT SIMS BAR-B-QUE

Have you ever been to a place where the sauce is so good, you just want to soak your bread in it? Sim's vinegar mustard brown sugar sauce is just that good. Started in 1937, Sim's Bar-B-Que is one of the very few black-owned businesses that survived integration. The original location on Thirty-third Street was the lunch time favorite for people from all walks of life. Today Sim's has several sites throughout the city and even offers catering. Ronald Settlers owns the Broadway restaurant and is responsible for the incorporation of the business. At the Broadway location you will find the same crowd that frequented the original restaurant, plus a few new faces. Known for their spare ribs and pork or beef sandwiches, Sim's is the place to go when you want good barbecue with a flavor unique to Little Rock.

2415 S. Broadway St., Little Rock
501-372-6868

1307 John Barrow Rd., Little Rock
501-224-2057

7601 Geyer Springs Rd., Little Rock
501-562-8844

simsbbqar.com

SIT ON THE DECK
AT CAJUN'S WHARF

If the weather is right, you want to sit on the deck. Trust me. It's like being on top of the world! Cajun's Wharf has it all: a three-level bar area with plenty of seating, good food, live music, and a stellar reputation. Here you can enjoy seafood or aged Angus beef, wine or a mixed cocktail, a late night party band or an early evening dinner. The choice is yours. Located behind the commercial warehouses along the waterfront, Cajun's also has great views of the Arkansas River. A couple of my favorite staples on the menu: Oysters Bienville, Boston Casserole, and the Play-De-Do! Check out their website to see what band is playing. Who knows? It may be a band you like. If not, the atmosphere will be so good that you won't notice the music! TRUST ME: DRINK THE PLAY-DE-DO!!

2400 Cantrell Rd., Little Rock
501-375-5351
cajunswharf.com

GO
TO SO

Ever had a fried green tomato crab cake? No? What are you waiting for? Go to SO! This intimate restaurant will have you bragging to your friends. The mellow ambiance is sure to relax your spirit. Tucked away between two of Little Rock's best neighborhoods, The Heights and Hillcrest, SO is the perfect blend of class and sophistication. When you get there, say hi to Theo, the longtime bartender who remembers everyone by name. Be sure to call for a reservation, as a table can be hard to come by. SO is well known for its food and service. In fact, the Sea Bass has never had a complaint! There is also a private lounge downstairs from the main dining room that can accommodate larger groups. Did we mention SO has a patio? And you never have to worry about the weather. SO has the capability to cover it completely if need be.

3610 Kavanaugh Blvd., Little Rock
501-663-1464
sorestaurantbar.com

TRY BUFFALO FISH
AT LASSIS INN

One of Arkansas's oldest restaurants, this iconic blue house serves up the best catfish and buffalo fish around. It has been featured in numerous media outlets for its deliciously simple menu. The fish is fried, hot, and served with a short list of side items. The setting is cozy inside the small house, with a jukebox by the front door, small wooden booths and tables, and walls covered with black history posters and clippings of reviews from magazines and newspapers.

518 E. 27th St., Little Rock
501-372-8714

If you like local dives check out these favorites:

Homer's
2517, 2001 E. Roosevelt Rd., Little Rock

Sandy's Homeplace Cafe
1710 E. 15th St., Little Rock

The Wing Shack
1407 John Barrow Rd., Little Rock

Bobby's Country Cookin'
301 N. Shackleford Rd. Ste. E1, Little Rock

DRINK WINE
AT ZIN WINE BAR

Zin is the place to be for wine connoisseurs. Their premium selection includes brands from all around the world. They offer forty wines by the glass and their quaint space makes it perfect for intimate conversation or a night out with friends. You can't go wrong with their wine flights; they come in both red and white varieties and offer three sensational selections. If you need something to accompany your beverage, the tapas menu offers a variety of options from gourmet nuts to stuffed pepadew peppers. For non-wine-drinkers, Zin also has an assortment of premium beers that are sure to satisfy. You also want to check to see if they have live music. Every once in a while you can catch a great local artist blessing the mic.

11121 N. Rodney Parham Rd., Little Rock
501-904-6988
zinlr.com

TAKE YOUR PICK
AT THE RIVER MARKET'S
OTTENHEIMER MARKET HALL

With so many choices and international flavors packed into one room, the River Market has an option for even the pickiest eater. Here you won't find fast food chains, but a true bazaar of international cuisine, from Little Rock residents, including Thai, Mexican, Middle Eastern, tastes of Tokyo, amazing burgers, bakery goods and sandwiches, Indian cuisine, pizza, Asian flavors, and of course, barbecue. Once you have decided what to eat, you can sit in the large seating area and log onto free Wi-Fi. The hall opens at 7 a.m., which makes it a good choice for breakfast, and does not close until 6 p.m. When you are done eating, pop into Shop the Rock and pick up some Little Rock souvenirs that will remind you of your trip for years to come.

400 President Clinton Ave., Little Rock
501-376-4781
rivermarket.info/eat

TIP
If you like choices, slide over to The Food Truck Stop at Station 801.
There is inside seating and something new every day!
Open Mon.-Fri. 11 a.m.-2:30 p.m.

801 Chester St., Little Rock, lrstation801.com

CREATE A SALAD
AT ZAZA'S FINE SALAD AND WOOD OVEN PIZZA

With several home-grown ingredients to choose from, ZAZA's is farm-to-table in true form. Create your own salad with your favorite toppings or simply pick one from the menu. Located in The Heights Neighborhood in Little Rock, ZAZA's is known for having one of the best salads in town. If you are looking for more than a salad, the wood oven pizza is made fresh with a few ingredients that ZAZA's takes pride in. According to their website, they are FANATICAL about certified San Marzano tomatoes and Molino Caputo Tipo 00, a true Italian doppio zero wheat flour. Want to know if those ingredients make a difference? Dare to be creative—pop into ZAZA's for a salad and pizza. For dessert, enjoy a serving of gelato, made fresh each morning.

5600 Kavanaugh Blvd., Ste. 100, Little Rock
501-661-9292
zazapizzaandsalad.com

PLAY
AT DAVE & BUSTER'S

Did you know Dave & Buster's has its roots right here in Little Rock? Original owners David Corriveau and James "Buster" Corley first operated bars in Little Rock called "Cash McCool's" and "Buster's." The two began their Dave & Buster's venture in Dallas in 1982. Now with over 110 locations, D&B offers state-of-the-art games, a huge menu, and full bar. They specialize in fun and it's a great spot to watch your favorite team on their big screens.

10900 Bass Pro Pkwy., Little Rock
501-777-3800
daveandbusters.com

TIP
Dave & Buster's is located at the Gateway Town Center and Outlets of Little Rock. You could spend the entire day there.

DINE
AT 42 BAR AND TABLE

Wondering why it's called 42? You guessed it! Arkansas is the birthplace of the forty-second President of the United States. A full-service restaurant, with simple but classy décor inside the William J. Clinton Presidential Library, 42 Bar and Table offers a variety of modern menu items and service fit for a president. It's the perfect backdrop for a business lunch or after work cocktail or dinner with friends. The outdoor seating area offers great views of the lighted pedestrian bridge, Arkansas River, and Riverfront Park. The most surprising thing about 42 is the prices. Not only is the food good, it's reasonable. The old adage, "you get what you pay for", does not apply to 42. Here you certainly get more.

1200 President Clinton Ave., Little Rock
501-537-0042
dineatfortytwo.com

EXPERIENCE ITALY
AT BRUNO'S LITTLE ITALY

Founded in Little Rock in 1949, Bruno's Little Italy has been serving authentic Neapolitan entrées for over fifty years. The restaurant has grown from its humble beginnings to a premier location in the heart of downtown. They were one of the first facilities to sign on to assist with the revitalization of Main Street, but it did not take others long to follow. It is this commitment to community that makes Bruno's a mainstay on the national culinary scene. A winner of several awards, including the Great Gold Cup Trophy of Honor for the best Italian food in the United States by Fair of Rome (tied with Mama Leone's in New York City), the Bruno family has succeeded in bringing a small piece of Italy to Arkansas.

310 Main St., Little Rock
501-372-7866
brunoslittleitaly.com

INDULGE
AT THE PANTRY

With locations in west Little Rock and the historic Hillcrest neighborhood, The Pantry West and The Pantry Crest offer Czech and German classics as well as delightful appetizers, burgers, salads, and flatbreads. The chefs expertly prepare items including house made bratwurst and Hungarian sausage, Lasagna al Forno, and paté. This place has quite the local following, so it's sure to delight the palate!

11404 N. Rodney Parham Rd., Little Rock
501-353-1875

722 N. Palm St., Little Rock
501-725-4945

littlerockpantry.com

FALL IN LOVE WITH SUSHI
AT KEMURI

Master Chef Greg Wallis has given Little Rock a taste of Tokyo. Kemuri has added something to the Little Rock food scene that is new and fresh. The self-proclaimed "best sushi in town" can be found here. Locals rave about the Crazy Monkey Roll, but traditional rolls are also available. If you are not a sushi lover, Kemuri doubles as a full-scale restaurant with traditional Japanese-style grilling. The Panang Curry will leave you raving. Located in one of Little Rock's most eclectic upscale neighborhoods, Kemuri shares the strip with several other local businesses. After dinner you can walk down the sidewalk for drinks Proof Bar + Lounge.

2601 Kavanaugh Blvd., Little Rock
501-660-4100
kemurirestaurant.com

ENJOY
WEEKEND BRUNCH
AT RED DOOR

Red Door's patio is the place to be for Saturday or Sunday brunch. Sometimes the wait is over an hour for the southern cuisine. What's so special about Red Door? It's the chef. Chef Mark Abernathy is a mainstay on the Little Rock food scene. He has been the face of many popular restaurants and now adds Red Door to his résumé. While most chefs view the kitchen as their workplace, Mark is different. He is active in the community and passionate about passing the art of cooking on to the next generation. He takes his skill into the world and tries to make a difference. You can taste his passion through his food at Red Door. Hint: If the line is long at Red Door, go next door to Loca Luna. Chef Abernathy is the mastermind behind it too.

3701 Old Cantrell Rd., Little Rock
501-666-8482
reddoorrestaurant.net

COOL OFF
AT LE POPS

Gone are the days when Popsicles were just Kool-Aid on a stick. Le Pops has transformed that simple concept into Popsicle heaven. Each treat is handmade with the best ingredients. Le Pops's bold and unusual flavors set them apart. Ever had Strawberry and Basil? Yeah, neither had we, but it's on the menu and it is amazing! They also serve vegan and non-dairy—this way everyone can enjoy a tasty treat. For those cold days, Le Pops even has Hot Pops. Imagine a chilled raspberry pop placed in a hot coffee, or a salted caramel pop soaked in hot chocolate. Le Pops has a variety of options. It's the perfect place for moms who are looking for healthy ice cream alternatives for themselves or their children.

5501 Kavanaugh Blvd., Little Rock
501-313-9558
lepops.com

SIT AROUND THE DINNER TABLE
AT CIAO BACI

Ciao Baci feels like home. What was once a nice bungalow in the Hillcrest neighborhood is now a comfortable restaurant. Complete with a porch swing, the atmosphere couldn't be more inviting. Specializing in service, Ciao Baci's goal is to make you feel like you are sharing a holiday meal with family. Don't let the name fool you, though, it is not an Italian restaurant. With a Mediterranean-inspired menu, there are a variety of interesting and innovative options from which to choose. The calamari and house sangria are their specialties. Enjoy either on the patio or the inside dining room. If you just want to stop in for a drink, happy hour is always happening—Ciao Baci is known for their drink specials.

605 Beechwood St., Little Rock
501-603-0238
ciaobaci.org

TIP
Want something sweet after dinner? Pop in next door to Izard Chocolate Factory for hand-crafted chocolates and caramels.
623 Beechwood St., Little Rock
501-352-5834, izardchocolate.com

RELIVE YOUR TEENAGE YEARS
AT PIZZA CAFE

Locals have kept this place in business for over twenty years. We love it, so much that servers know you by name and can deliver your order without even asking. We are convinced that if we still had sock hops, Pizza Cafe would be where teenagers would meet before and after. In fact, now forty-year-olds will sit around the establishment telling stories of their high school days at Pizza Cafe. It is the hole in the wall that sucks you in, and you keep coming back for more. More friendly service, more cold beer, and more pizza. All are welcomed at either location. The original location is on Rebsamen Park Road; those walls hold great memories of Arkansans from all walks of life.

1517 Rebsamen Park Rd., Little Rock
501-664-6133

14710 Cantrell Rd., Little Rock
501-868-2600

pizzacafelr.com

SATISFY YOUR SOUL
AT KITCHEN EXPRESS

Kitchen Express is soul food heaven. Serving up homemade rolls, smoked turkey legs, fried chicken, and barbecued ribs, this cafeteria-style restaurant is Little Rock's go-to for soul food. Lunch time at Kitchen Express is always busy. The love for the food and fast service brings together people from all walks of life. However, you don't want to miss out on the country-style breakfast. Where else can you get biscuits and gravy and smothered potatoes at the drive-through? Kitchen Express also caters and has a banquet room for those who have large numbers to feed.

4600 Asher Ave., Little Rock
501-663-3500
thekitchenexpress.com

After you eat, enjoy urban adult nightlife nearby!

La'Changes
3325 W. Roosevelt Rd., Little Rock
501-661-9810

Trois
4314 Asher Ave., Little Rock
501-663-7800

Jazzi's
5200 Asher Ave., Little Rock
501-562-6919

Club Envy
7200 Colonel Glenn Rd., Little Rock
501-569-9113

Club Elevations
7200 Colonel Glenn Rd., Little Rock
501-562-3317

Sway
412 Louisiana St., Little Rock
501-777-5428
clubsway.com

Triniti
1021 Jessie Rd., Little Rock
501-664-2744

Discovery
1021 Jessie Rd., Little Rock
501-664-4784

Electric Cowboy
9515 I-30, Little Rock
501-562-6000

Photo provided courtesy of
Little Rock Convention & Visitors Bureau.

CHAT WITH A FRIEND
AT COMMUNITY BAKERY

The name says it all. This is the community's bakery. The place for the people. And it has been since 1947. We're convinced that some major business deals have been signed within these four walls. Community Bakery is where both business professionals and artists meet. Thanks to Ralph Hinson, the company's founder, for his vision. Although the first location was in North Little Rock, it moved to the capital city in 1952. Today, it's owned by Joe Fox and while it has two Little Rock locations, the Main Street bakery remains the heart of the business. Community Bakery is where Arkansans go to chat with friends!

1200 Main St., Little Rock
501-375-6418

270 S. Shackleford Rd., Little Rock
501-224-1656

communitybakery.com

TIP
Check out Rock Town Distillery right across the street. It's Arkansas's first legal distillery since prohibition. They offer great tours and tastings!
rocktowndistillery.com

MUSIC AND ENTERTAINMENT

CATCH A PERFORMANCE
AT ROBINSON PERFORMANCE HALL

This historic performance hall has served as the place in Little Rock for all things music, dance, and theater since 1939. Robinson has been home to many greats including Elvis Presley, Ella Fitzgerald, Gene Autry, Glenn Campbell, Aretha Franklin, and Nat King Cole. In 2014 the facility closed to undergo a $70 million renovation. The all-new Robinson reopened to great fanfare in November 2016. Little Rock's landmark performing arts facility returned better than ever. Home to the Arkansas Symphony Orchestra, Broadway Theater Series, and Ballet Arkansas, the facility also plays host to countless concerts, performances, dances, and special events. If you are looking for a place to host a meeting, Robinson's all new conference center offers some of the best views of the Arkansas River in its grand ballroom with large glass windows, or via the sizeable outside terrace.

426 W. Markham St., Little Rock
501-376-4781
robinsoncenter.com

SPEND A DAY
AT THE ARKANSAS STATE FAIR

If you are looking for fun for the whole family or just an adult outing, in October of every year, the Arkansas State Fair has it all. This is not some fly-by-night carnival with impossible-to-win games, this is the real deal. Complete with livestock shows, pageants, and concerts, there is something for everyone. If you are looking for southern-fried desserts, look no further. They fry anything from Oreos to Twinkes! You can also enjoy a turkey leg or a foot-long corndog, both made with special down south love. Aside from entertainment and southern-fried cuisine, the Arkansas State Fair is also committed to providing educational opportunities. Thanks to the Arkansas Livestock Association, an organization committed to youth development, here you can learn about agriculture, livestock, and technology. The Arkansas State Fair makes Little Rock the place to be in October!

2600 Howard St., Little Rock
501-372-8341
arkansasstatefair.com

LAUGH
AT THE LOONY BIN COMEDY CLUB

Little Rock is certainly delighted to be one of only four cities where the Loony Bin Comedy Club brings laughter. (The other locations are Wichita, Tulsa, and Oklahoma City.) Sometimes you need a break from the bar scene and movie theaters, and Loony Bin provides the city with a funny alternative. It is not uncommon to catch some great up-and-coming comedians as well as the legends. You can also enjoy dinner or appetizers while you laugh. Loony Bin is perfect for date night or hanging with friends. Either way you are sure to laugh until your stomach hurts! Check their website or call for show times and to find out which comedian is on the bill. You can pay at the door, but we don't recommend it as this place is always sold out!

10301 N. Rodney Parham Rd., Little Rock
501-228-5555
loonybincomedy.com

SEE BIG SCREEN FUN
AT FILMLAND

The Arkansas Cinema Society's Filmland is a curated annual celebration of cinema! Filmland hosts producers, writers, actors and directors, production designers, cinematographers, etc. to help showcase their work. Screenings are followed by an in depth on-stage Q&A conversation led by ACS founder and filmmaker Jeff Nichols. Every August, Filmland features a collection of curated films and television shows as well as a selection of Arkansas films—either made by an Arkansan or made in Arkansas. During Filmland, the ACS also hosts Happy Hour networking events and RAD after-parties to celebrate the growing film culture in Arkansas. The ACS hosts year-round events to achieve its mission to nurture and inspire filmmakers in Arkansas, but the annual Filmland is any movie lover's paradise.

501-376-4781
info@arkansascinemasociety.org
arkansascinemasociety.org

TIP
Agasi 7: Rooftop Bar + Kitchen is a great place for an after show drink or meal.
322 Rock St., Little Rock, 501-244-0044

LIGHT UP THE NIGHT
WITH RIVER LIGHTS IN THE ROCK

Check out Little Rock's skyline in the evening with the glow of thousands of LED lights reflecting off the Arkansas River when three downtown bridges illuminate. The Main Street, Junction, and Clinton Presidential Park bridges add color, vibrancy, and life to the capital city skyline each night. Sometimes the lights represent special events or holidays, other evenings, just random arrays of color fill the bridge spans. Take a walk through Riverfront Park to experience the lights up close.

400 President Clinton Ave., Little Rock
riverlightsintherock.com

TIP
If you want a little something sweet to take on your stroll through the River Lights, stop by Kilwins in the River Market for ice cream, chocolates, and handmade treats.
415 President Clinton Ave., Little Rock
501-379-9865
kilwins.com/stores/kilwins-little-rock

Interesting Fact:
Little Rock and North Little Rock are Arkansas's
twin cities separated by the Arkansas River.
Although many think the two are the same,
they are, in fact, two different cities.

EAT GREEK
AT THE INTERNATIONAL
GREEK FOOD FESTIVAL

Okay. I have a confession. I played professional basketball in Greece. After my career was over, I thought I'd have to return to the country to find authentic Greek food. Boy, was I wrong! May 2014, I attended my first International Greek Food Festival in Little Rock at the Annunciation Greek Orthodox Church. Immediately I marked the 2015 date on my calendar. This festival is the largest ethnic festival in Arkansas. Here you can find gyros, souvlaki, and of course, baklava. To go with the traditional Mediterranean cuisine, you can also enjoy authentic music and dance, and even tour the church if you choose. This festival is perfect for family fun. If you decide that you do not want to hang out, don't worry, there is a drive-through line. The International Greek Food Festival is all about the food.

1100 Napa Valley Dr., Little Rock
501-221-5300
greekfoodfest.com

TIP
Looking for Greek anytime of the year?
Try Layla's Gyros, Taziki's Mediterranean Café, or Leo's Greek Castle
laylasgyro.com, tazikiscafe.com

Other Food Festivals to Attend

Jewish Food and Cultural Festival
jewisharkansas.org/jewish-food-and-cultural-festival

World Cheese Dip Championship
cheesedip.net

Arkansas Cornbread Festival
arkansascornbreadfestival.com

Main Street Food Truck Festival
mainstreetfoodtrucks.com

IndiaFest
indiafestar.com

LINE DANCE
AT ELECTRIC COWBOY

From salsa dancing to old fashioned boot scoot boogie, you can find it all at Electric Cowboy. A southern favorite with locations in Tennessee, Georgia, Texas, and Arkansas, the Arkansas clubs are the only ones located in the Midwest. Thursday night is Boots and Buckles night, where the fashion is quite impressive. Pull out your favorite pair of boots and your most striking buckle and come enjoy a drink and good ole country line dancing. Wednesday night is salsa night with $3 Coronas and margaritas all night long! If you are not a dancer, join in the Thursday night pool tournament. Remember, you must be twenty-one to enter, doors open at 8 p.m., and the Electric Cowboy has a license to stay open until 5 a.m.!

9515 I-30, Little Rock
501-562-6000
electriccowboy.com/littlerock

DIVE IN
AT MIDTOWN BILLIARDS

The folks at Midtown may not know you, but they will treat you like family. A private club that will offer you a membership at the door, make no mistake, Midtown is a dive and a good one. This eclectic spot is where you go to play a game of pool or bottle toss and have a cold one. Here you can just be you! However, don't expect linen tablecloths and fancy wine glasses, neither would last a week. Happy hour is 3-8 p.m. where they offer fifty cents off all drinks. Midtown is also where you can find the best burger in town after 2 a.m. Their grill is open until 4:30 a.m., and the doors don't close until 5 a.m.

1316 Main St., Little Rock
501-372-9990
midtownar.com

TIP
Bottle toss is a big deal here. It happens every Thursday at 7 p.m. Get there early!

CATCH A MOVIE
IN THE PARK

What better way to enjoy a movie than in the beautiful Arkansas weather, cuddled under a blanket with family? As a part of the River Market programming, Movies in the Park is a public event for all to enjoy. The First Security Amphitheater opens an hour before show time, and the movies begin at sundown. If you thought you liked drive-in theaters, you will love watching a film under the stars. The best thing about Movies in the Park is, it's free. According to their website, "The mission of Movies in the Park is help foster a sense of community and enjoyment in downtown Little Rock and throughout Central Arkansas by bringing people together to enjoy a movie in a unique setting along the scenic banks of the Arkansas River." It doesn't get much better than that.

400 President Clinton Ave., Little Rock
501-375-2552
moviesintheparklr.net

Raining? Catch a movie indoors!

Rave Cinemark
18 Colonel Glenn Plaza Dr., Little Rock
501-678-0499
cinemark.com

Regal Breckenridge
1200 Breckenridge Dr., Little Rock
501-224-0990
regmovies.com

Chenal 9 IMAX
17825 Chenal Pkwy., Little Rock
501-821-2616
bbtheatres.com

Riverdale 10 VIP Cinema
2600 Cantrell Rd., Little Rock
501-296-9955
riverdale10.com

Movie Tavern Gateway Town Center
11300 Bass Pro Pkwy., Little Rock
501-319-6799
movietavern.com/locations/littlerock

WATCH
A LIVE PERFORMANCE
AT THE ARKANSAS REPERTORY THEATRE

Affectionately known as The Rep, the Arkansas Repertory Theatre has been the backdrop for nonprofit professional theater since 1976. This is not the place to go for the local annual holiday play. The Rep produces high-quality theater with professionals working both behind the scenes and on stage. The productions are more than just entertaining; they are reflections of the highest artistic standards. The Rep is also invested in the next generation through their arts in education programs across Arkansas, where they reach upwards of 12,000 young people each year. Check their website to see what productions the new season will bring. In the past *Les Misérables, Hairspray, Hamlet*, and a host of other classics have been on the bill. Whatever the current season brings, we can guarantee it will be spectacular.

601 Main St., Little Rock
501-378-0405, therep.org

TIP
Grab a bite to eat before the show at Three Fold Noodles + Dumpling Co. located right next door. You will not be disappointed.
eat3fold.com

PAINT WITH A TWIST
AT PAINTING WITH A TWIST

Sometimes you want something different. Painting with a Twist brings you just that. Whether it's a fun night on the town with friends or a romantic evening, this artistic venue will get your creative juices flowing. The concept began as Corks and Canvas in 2007, but evolved into Painting with a Twist in 2009. Here's how it works: first you visit the website or call to get a schedule of which paintings are being taught on what nights, then you pick a night and make a reservation, and finally you show up with your drink of choice (Painting with a Twist is BYOB) and paint! There are two Central Arkansas locations, each with different options. If you prefer a private party where you can choose the art you make, Painting with a Twist will accommodate.

400 N. Bowman Rd., Ste. 32, Little Rock
501-410-4422

4178 E. McCain Blvd., North Little Rock
501-352-1366

paintingwithatwist.com

SING FAVORITE TUNES
AT WILLY D'S PIANO BAR

Who doesn't love a good piano bar? When you combine two musicians going back and forth, there is no way to avoid hearing your favorite tune. We all know once you hear it, you can't help but sing along! Willy D's is very popular, so there is never a dull night. With two full-service bars and a full kitchen, you can eat and drink all you want. They are open 7 p.m.-2 a.m. Tuesday-Saturday. Happy hour is all night on Tuesday and ladies' night is Friday, no cover all night long. Just in case you go on a Friday or Saturday and you want to turn things up a notch, dance venue Club Deep is right downstairs, so you can get your party on!

322 President Clinton Ave., Little Rock
501-244-9550
willydspianobar.com

TIP
Pianists not playing your style music? No sweat.
There is another piano bar, Ernie Biggs, right across the street.

LISTEN TO FREE TUNES
AT JAZZ IN THE PARK

Jazz in the Park celebrates local musicians with free concerts each Wednesday evening in April and September. They take place in the History Pavilion in Riverfront Park.

400 President Clinton Ave., Little Rock
501-320-3503
rivermarket.info

More rockin' live music spots

Stickyz Rock and Roll Chicken Shack
107 River Market Ave., Little Rock
501-372-7707
stickyz.com

Vino's
923 W. 7th St., Little Rock
501-375-8466
vinosbrewpub.com

Discovery Night Club
1021 Jessie Rd., Little Rock
501-664-4784
latenightdisco.com

The White Water Tavern
2500 W. 7th St., Little Rock
501-375-8400
whitewatertavern.com

Cajun's Wharf
2400 Cantrell Rd., Little Rock
501-375-5351
cajunswharf.com

Visit arkansaslivemusic.com for a master schedule!

FIND YOUR FAVORITE BEER
AT FLYING SAUCER

You name it, they've got it. With over seventy-five beers on the draft wall and one hundred and fifty in the bottle, Flying Saucer aims to satisfy every taste. Beer snobs love this place. The Little Rock franchise is a large venue with lots of room, so not only can you host a special event, you can sit comfortably and try any beer you'd like. They also have a great menu of bar food and a pool room in the basement. Regular events include trivia night on Tuesday, with two rounds starting at 7:30 p.m. and 10 p.m. Wednesday night is brewery night. If you purchase a specialty beer, you keep the glass. Are you really beer crazy? Join the UFO club and keep track of every beer you drink!

323 President Clinton Ave., Little Rock
501-372-8032
beerknurd.com/locations/little-rock-flying-saucer

TIP
If you find yourself in downtown Little Rock on the second Friday of the month, check out 2FAN (2nd Friday Art Night). The evening celebrates local artists and galleries.
2ndfridayartnight.org

HAVE A PICNIC
AT MURRAY PARK

When was the last time you had a good old-fashioned picnic? One where you pack lunch and a blanket and sit on the ground? If it wasn't just yesterday, that's too long. Complete with a fishing stream, bike trails, and picnic tables, this is the perfect place to rekindle your love for picnics. Located alongside the river, it has eight pavilions, three soccer fields, a boat dock, and play areas. Locals often use it for family reunions and company picnics. In the warmer months, Murray is a popular place for fishing tournaments. Murray is also pet friendly, offering a fenced, off-leash dog park where your four-legged friends can have fun as well.

5900 Rebsamen Park Rd., Little Rock
501-371-4770

SIP GRAND HIGH TEA
AT EMPRESS OF LITTLE ROCK

Grand High Tea at the Empress is taken directly from the Victorian era. History tells us that Victorian High Tea was a more formal experience complete with scones and finger sandwiches. There was also a traditional table setting and plenty of rules of etiquette to go around. The Empress has taken a cue from the best. Their Grand High Tea is a replica of history. Tea is served in the formal dining room and everything is handmade on-site. When tea is done, take a tour of one of the most traditional bed and breakfasts in the United States. Remember to call and make a reservation for tea. It only happens on Sundays, and space is limited.

2120 S. Louisiana St., Little Rock
501-347-7966
theempress.com

SPORTS AND RECREATION

WALK, RUN, OR BIKE
ACROSS THE BIG DAM BRIDGE

Little Rock is home to the longest pedestrian and bicycle bridge in North America built specifically for that purpose. It really is a big damn bridge. Ninety feet above the Arkansas River and 4,226 feet long, it's a hot spot for both cyclists and pedestrians. Once you make it to the center, the view is magical. You can use the built-in binoculars to bird-watch, or sit on the bench and soak in nature. The Big Dam Bridge is perfect for exercise enthusiasts. What better way to clear your mind than to jog across the bridge? The lights along the bridge make it a spectacular view from afar. The Society of American Travel Writers named the bridge, "one of North America's Top Ten Bridge Sites." Each year the foundation hosts the Big Dam Bridge 100 Bicycle Tour. (Arkansas's largest cycling event.) To learn more about this event visit bigdambridge100.com.

7700 Rebsamen Park Rd., Little Rock
501-340-6800
bigdambridge.com

RESERVE A LANE
AT DUST BOWL LANES & LOUNGE

This retro-inspired tribute to the bowling alleys and lounges of the 1970s is sure to be fun for everyone. The Dust Bowl isn't just about bowling. It's a unique entertainment destination that can accommodate a variety of parties and special events, or just a night out with friends. Frequent visitor to Little Rock? Join their loyalty program for deals and discounts. Come hungry because they have an extensive menu and full bar to keep you fueled. The street tacos are definitely worth a try. If you want to keep the party going, hop next door to Fassler Hall. It's an authentic German Beer Hall, known for its beer, brunch, and live entertainment!

315 E. Capitol Ave., Little Rock
501-353-0775
dustbowllounge.com/locations/little-rock

TIP
You can find more bowling at Professor Bowl located at 901 Towne Oaks Dr., Little Rock.

· ·

CHEER ON
THE ARKANSAS TRAVELERS

Minor league baseball is a big deal in Little Rock. Arkansas is a state with no NBA, NFL, or MLB franchises, so we love what we have—collegiate sports and minor league baseball. We take both seriously. Dickey Stephens Park, home to the Travelers, is not your average minor league field. The design is spectacular, without a bad seat in the house. It is also well-kept, and is always nice and clean. In the distance you can see the skyline of the city, which gives it a special appeal. On game day, just like in the majors, there is a lot of fun for the kids and crowd participation. With the beer garden and free Wi-Fi, you can actually attend a game and have a blast without watching baseball at all! Perfect family outing.

400 W. Broadway St., North Little Rock
501-664-1555
travs.com

SHOOT HOOPS WITH THE LITTLE ROCK TROJANS
AT UA LITTLE ROCK

Thanks to Derek Fisher for helping put his college home on the map! The Trojans of the University of Arkansas at Little Rock were once the former NBA standout's team, but now they are Little Rock's team. While the college has a plethora of sports, basketball has become a city favorite. The fifty-six-hundred-seat Jack Stephens Center, where both the men and women play, is perfect for the midsized college. The Trojans compete in the Sun Belt conference, which includes Arkansas State, another Arkansas college, located in Jonesboro. Needless to say, this game is always exciting. A Trojans basketball game is the perfect family event. They consistently finish at the top of the conference in both men's and women's basketball, easily making them both exciting to watch.

2801 S. University Ave., Little Rock
501-565-8257
lrtrojans.com

TAKE YOUR BEST FRIEND
TO BARK BAR

Traveling with your four-legged, furry friend? Little Rock is home to Arkansas's first indoor/outdoor off-leash venue catering exclusively to dogs and their owners. Located in a once vacant Mission-style church in the South Main (SoMa) District, the play area and bar provide a fun place for people to hang out with their pets, and meet others in an entertaining and very social atmosphere. Specialty menu items include snacks, coffees, brews and cocktails for the humans, as well as creative canine cuisine. You don't have to have a dog to visit, but if you do bring one, be sure to bring their shot records, they are required for entry.

1201 S. Spring St., Little Rock
501-295-3989
barkbar.com

TIP

Check out these great dog parks for more
fun with Fido.
MacArthur Unleashed Dog Park
601 E. 9th St., Little Rock

Murray Dog Park
5900 Rebsamen Park Rd., Little Rock

SLIDE
AT WILD RIVER COUNTRY

It's no secret that summers in Arkansas are hot. Wild River Country is where people go to cool off! They travel from all over the state to enjoy the water park. The Wave Pool is a longtime favorite for many, but recent expansions have given the park a boost. Wild River Country features twelve rides and has options for all age groups. Smaller children can hang out in the Tad Pool, or drift in the Sidewinder with mom and dad. For those who are a bit more daring, the Thrilling 3 and the Vortex will satisfy your thrill. Anyone can enjoy the good Ole' Swimmin' Hole. Aside from fun, Wild River Country is also affordable. Admission for children two and under is free and they offer military discounts.

6820 Crystal Hill Rd., North Little Rock
501-753-8600
wildrivercountry.com

BIKE
THE ARKANSAS RIVER TRAIL

The Arkansas River Trail is perfect for biking or running. Outdoor enthusiasts will love the beautiful Arkansas scenery. The trail runs alongside the river and has multiple points of access. There are also bike repair stations, restrooms, and information stops along the trail, making it extremely user friendly. The trail welcomes pets as well, but they must be leashed at all times and you must pick up their waste. Just in case you are a horse lover, the Arkansas River Trail features horseback riding trails in Burns Park in North Little Rock and Two Rivers Park in Little Rock.

Not traveling with a bike? Don't worry, you can rent one in Little Rock's River Market District.

arkansasrivertrail.org

CHILL LIKE A ROYAL
AT THE CASTLE ON STAGECOACH

Whether you are a Prince or a Princess, there is a carriage ride waiting just for you. The Castle on Stagecoach is one of Little Rock's best gems and Arkansas's only castle venue. If you are just looking to chill on a Sunday afternoon, head there for brunch. Not only will you find great food, but music, drinks, and a chance to roam around the Castle also await you. Keep an eye on their website for the Princess Tea Parties; they host them throughout the year and it's all the craze at local playgrounds. With both indoor and outdoor space, it's the perfect place for a small, intimate event or a life-changing celebration. The next time you are looking to chill, visit the Castle at Stagecoach; it's sure to make you feel like royalty.

6601 Stagecoach Rd., Little Rock
501-960-0658
castleonstagecoach.com

ROLL ON THE RIVER
USING A SEGWAY

Tina Turner isn't the only one rolling on the river; you can too with 404 Tour Co.'s Segway Tours. A Segway is a two-wheeled self-balancing device (think hover board with handlebars), and a great way to tour the riverfront and River Market area. Before you can take off, you must complete a training session. The goal is to be sure everyone is totally comfortable before riding. Although the Segway can only travel about twelve miles per hour, helmets are required. Safety is first! The tour normally lasts about ninety minutes, taking you past Little Rock's best attractions. Tours are narrated by a tour guide, and can be customized.

404 E. 3rd St., Little Rock
501-747-9544
404tour.com

CLIMB
PINNACLE MOUNTAIN

Arkansas is famous for its state parks. If you haven't visited at least one, you are missing out. They don't call it the Natural State for nothing! Pinnacle Mountain State Park is located west of Little Rock and was the first near a metropolitan area. While the park features hiking and mountain bike trails, its most popular feature is Pinnacle Mountain. You will find all kinds of people at Pinnacle Mountain. Some run up it to stay in shape, while others hike slowly. With two separate trails, you have your choice of taking the East Summit, which is more rugged, or the less rocky West Summit. Whichever you choose, the view from the top will be well worth the climb.

11901 Pinnacle Valley Rd., Little Rock
501-868-5806
arkansasstateparks.com/pinnaclemountain

TIP
If you want more rocky terrain check out Rattlesnake Ridge just west of Pinnacle Mountain. The area protects several rare plant and animal species and is one of the most dramatic rocky summits in the eastern Ouachita Mountains.

STROLL THE JUNCTION BRIDGE
PEDESTRIAN WALKWAY

We love our Little Rock bridges. All of them are well-lit at night, giving the city an ambiance like no other. Aside from how beautiful they look through the windows of downtown hotels, they also can help enhance a romantic evening. After enjoying a meal in the River Market District, you can head to the Junction Bridge Pedestrian Walkway, which extends across the Arkansas River between Little Rock and North Little Rock. Both cities saw the importance of making the bridge user-friendly in 2001, and along with Pulaski County and the Arkansas Department of Transportation, made strides to do so. Today the bridge, complete with elevators and benches, offers pedestrians and bike riders yet another unique way to enjoy Little Rock.

200 Ottenheimer Plaza, Little Rock
501-374-3001
pulaskicounty.net/junction-bridge

CREATE YOUR OWN
"WISH YOU WERE HERE" POSTCARD

Once you are done spending time atop the Junction Bridge, take the stairs or elevator down and take a picture through one of Little Rock's human postcard frames. These are life size photo frames that read, "Greetings from Little Rock. Wish you were here!" It's simple: you stand behind one, snap a photo with the landmark in the background, and there you have it, your own picture postcard! Up for a challenge? See if you can find all three! There is one at the Junction Bridge, one under the Interstate 30 bridge overlooking the Clinton Presidential Library, and the final one near the Big Dam Bridge. When you snap your photo, don't forget to upload and share on social media! Use #WishYouWereHere and #LittleRock. Contact the Little Rock Convention & Visitors Bureau for more information.

Little Rock Convention & Visitors Bureau
501-376-4781

RUN
THE LITTLE ROCK MARATHON

During marathon weekend in Little Rock, everyone is engaged. As a runner, you will not find a city that supports its marathon more than Little Rock. People line the streets, cheering on perfect strangers and offering beverages to the athletes. If you'd like, you can even purchase an Outrageous VIP Experience which will turn the southern hospitality up a notch. The Little Rock Marathon is known for its extreme themes and out-of-this-world gigantic finisher medals. It is a Boston Qualifier which attracts people from all over the world who flood the streets for a chance to qualify for the big race. Just like any other city, Little Rock offers a half marathon, a 10K, a 5K run/walk, and a kid's marathon.

500 W. Markham St., Room 109, Little Rock
littlerockmarathon.com

GET HIGH
AT ALTITUDE TRAMPOLINE PARK OR THIRD REALM EXTREME AIR SPORTS

Not the kind of high that will land you in rehab, but the fun kind of high-flying experience you get from over two hundred interconnected trampolines or partaking in extreme air sports. The name says it all at Altitude Trampoline Park. Altitude is a huge open space with trampolines of all kinds where you can dunk like the pros or flip like the Olympians. But be careful, when you come in you have to sign a waiver, so in the event that you don't land your double back handspring like the pros, you pay the hospital bill. To be safe, have fun in the foam pit or play dodgeball. For smaller children, there is a Kids Zone for jumpers under eighty pounds. For the extreme thrill seeker, head over to Third Realm and work your way through the ninja obstacle course, trapeze, or bounce on the angled wall trampolines. Got little ones, they also have an area for kids six and under in the KidJump area. Check out their website for fun themed nights and special events.

15707 Chanel Pkwy., Little Rock
501-353-1281
altitudetrampolineparklr.com

4711 Talley Rd., Little Rock
501-313-0100
3rdrealm.us

SKATE
AT ARKANSAS SKATIUM

Looking for family fun or a unique date? Take a figure skating class at Arkansas Skatium. If you are only in town for a short while, they offer a drop-in session for $12 for the general public; for those who reside in Central Arkansas there is a regular schedule of lessons. If the ice is too cold, slide over to the roller side. Arkansas Skatium has both! In fact, you can pop in and skate on both during public skating times for $10-$20 depending on the package you choose. Because it is also home to the Diamond Edge Figure Skating Club, it hosts competitions from time to time, so be sure to call or check the website before you visit.

1311 Bowman Rd., Little Rock
501-227-4333
arkansasskatium.com

LEARN AND PLAY
AT RIVERFRONT PARK

This is no ordinary public park. Gone are the swings, merry-go-rounds, and sandboxes. They have been replaced with underground tunnels, large climbing stones, a motion-sensor spray pad, and yes, even a sculpture garden. This is a park of the twenty-first century. It was designed to inspire imagination and discovery while encouraging innovative thinking. Riverfront Park as a whole features the Clinton Presidential Park Bridge, Little Rock Civil War Marker, Riverfront History Pavilion, Junction Bridge, Vogel Schwartz Sculpture Garden, Peabody Splash Park, Medical Mile, William E. "Bill" Clark Wetlands, First Security Amphitheater, Witt Stephens Jr. Central Arkansas Nature Center, Ozark Pavilion, Rotary Plaza, and the La Petite Roche Plaza, our city's namesake. The entire park spans eleven blocks, and thirty-three acres, along the banks of the Arkansas River. There's something for everyone at Riverfront Park, and the Peabody Splash Park is a great way for the little ones to cool off after enjoying the nature center and our dynamic sculpture garden. If the splash pad is too busy with big kids, take the little ones to the children's splash fountain located behind the Marriott hotel on the west end of the park.

202 La Harpe Blvd., Little Rock
501-375-2552, rivermarket.info

DO IT YOURSELF
AT THE PAINTED PIG

What does an ambitious young college grad do when she finds out her neighborhood art studio is closing? She starts her own. That's exactly what Allie Nottingham did in 2007. During her final semester at the University of Central Arkansas, The Painted Pig was born and since then it has kept growing. Today, not only can you make your own pottery, you can purchase pre-painted art-related gifts and design your own jewelry. The Painted Pig is the perfect place to host a group. During girls' night out sessions, you can even bring in beer and wine. A lot of school-aged artists enjoy hosting birthday parties here as well. Visit their website for pricing and other information.

5622 R St., Little Rock
501-280-0553
paintedpigstudio.com

TIP
If you don't have dinner plans give Heights Taco & Tamale Co. a try. It's right around the corner and the food is amazing!
5805 Kavanaugh Blvd., Little Rock
501-313-4848

Photo provided courtesy of
Little Rock Convention & Visitors Bureau.

Just in Case You Love to Golf

War Memorial Park
5110 W. Markham St., Little Rock
501-663-0854
littlerock.org/ParksRecreation/golfcourses

Hindman Park
60 Brookview Dr., Little Rock
501-565-6450
littlerock.org/ParksRecreation/golfcourses

Rebsamen Golf Course
3400 Rebsamen Park Rd., Little Rock
501-666-7965
littlerock.org/ParksRecreation/golfcourses

First Tee of Arkansas
First Tee Way, Little Rock
501-562-4635
thefirstteear.org

Big Rock Mini Golf and Fun Park
11411 Baseline Rd., Little Rock
501-455-3750
bigrockfunpark.com

Photo provided courtesy of
Little Rock Convention & Visitors Bureau.

LITTLE ROCK CENTRAL HIGH SCH

CULTURE AND HISTORY

GET YOUR PASSPORT STAMPED
AT THE WILLIAM J. CLINTON
PRESIDENTIAL LIBRARY AND MUSEUM

The William J. Clinton Presidential Center and Park includes the University of Arkansas Clinton School of Public Service, the Presidential Library, and the Little Rock offices of the Clinton Foundation. At the library you can view the complete archives of the Clinton presidency through permanent exhibits together with an exact replica of the Oval Office and the Cabinet Room as well as temporary exhibits. The library is a true testament to President Clinton's desire to demonstrate sustainable design and practices. The facility boasts a Platinum LEED (Leadership in Energy and Environmental Design) designation. When you are done witnessing history, have lunch at 42 Bar and Table, the full-service restaurant on-site, catch a lecture at the Clinton School featuring world-renowned leaders and relevant topics, or explore the park surrounding the library. The park features wetlands, the Presidential Park Bridge, and the Anne Frank Tree. The center also has plenty of event space for private dinners, receptions, or educational lectures. You can also find out more about Little Rock's history through the audio tours.

1200 President Clinton Ave., Little Rock
501-374-4242, clintonpresidentialcenter.org

CONDUCT AN EXPERIMENT
AT THE MUSEUM OF DISCOVERY

Children and adults can find their inner scientist at the Museum of Discovery. Opened in 1927, MOD is Arkansas's oldest museum and today is the state's premiere science center featuring over ninety hands-on experiments. Crowd favorites include Tornado Alley Theater and the bed of nails. Most recently, the Museum of Discovery acquired the Guinness World Record musical bi-polar Tesla coil that produces two hundred thousand volts of electricity. Ranked sixth-best US science museum by MENSA International IQ Society, it's not just for the kiddos, the Science After Dark programming is all about adult fun. MOD has also made its way to the national stage, featured on Jimmy Fallon multiple times.

500 President Clinton Ave., Little Rock
501-396-7050
museumofdiscovery.org

DISCOVER HISTORY
AT THE LITTLE ROCK CENTRAL HIGH SCHOOL NATIONAL HISTORIC SITE

In history books across the world, students read about the 1957 desegregation crisis at Central High School. The story of nine African American students—Ernest Green, Elizabeth Eckford, Jefferson Thomas, Terrence Roberts, Carlotta Walls LaNier, Minniejean Brown, Gloria Ray Karlmark, Thelma Mothershed, and Melba Pattillo Beals—who marched into the then all-white Central High School, made national headlines. The Little Rock Nine, as the group has since been called, became the faces of integration and symbols of progress. The complete archive of their story, including video, narratives, and exhibits, can be found on-site. Many of the civil rights legends still have strong connections to the center. Who knows? Maybe you will get to shake hands with one of them! Or better yet, listen to them recount events of 1957 in their own words. Little Rock Central High is also included as a top ten landmark site along the US Civil Rights Trail.

2120 W. Daisy L Gatson Bates Dr., Little Rock
501-374-1957
nps.gov/chsc
civilrightstrail.com

After you learn about how it all started, visit Little Rock's Historically Black Colleges and Universities. They are rich with tradition and history.

Philander Smith College
900 W. Daisy L Gatson Bates Dr., Little Rock
501-375-9845
philander.edu

Arkansas Baptist College
1621 Dr. Martin Luther King Dr., Little Rock
501-420-1200
arkansasbaptist.edu

Shorter College
604 N. Locust St., North Little Rock
501-374-6305
shortercollege.edu

TIP
Want to go deeper? Visit arkansascivilrightsheritage.org/civil-rights-trail for more information on the Arkansas Civil Rights Trail. Also visit the sculpture, *Testaments*, located on the grounds of the Arkansas State Capitol. It vividly portrays the members of the Little Rock Nine during their high school days.

EXPLORE A RESTORED ANTEBELLUM HOME
AT HISTORIC ARKANSAS MUSEUM

The history of Little Rock begins here at the Historic Arkansas Museum. The history and culture of Arkansas is celebrated through exhibits, collections, and research. Visitors can explore restored antebellum homes on their original block or learn the history of the Bowie Knife. They can also view collections of art, furniture, pottery, quilts, and jewelry all made by Arkansans. There is also a body of original documents including census records, business ledgers, and newspapers. Historic Arkansas Museum also offers annual family events, day camps, and field trip programs. It's the perfect place to bring school children of all ages, as they have special programming tailored for each grade level. Once you are done learning history here, stop by the Museum of Discovery for a little science. The two are very close to each other.

200 E. 3rd St., Little Rock
501-324-9351
historicarkansas.org

HELP CHANGE THE WORLD
AT HEIFER INTERNATIONAL

It's difficult to describe an organization like Heifer in just a few words. The work that they do worldwide is well-respected and important—and the home office, a beautiful platinum-green building, is in Little Rock, just off Interstate 30. Heifer International is certainly doing its part to make the world a better place. Their mission is simple—to end hunger and poverty—and they are doing so one farm animal at a time. Heifer's systematic model for bringing about the transformation of impoverished economies by giving families farm animals has proven to be effective. The animals not only provide food, but also a way to make an income from the sale of the products they produce. Heifer has a strong presence in Africa, Nepal, Haiti, and throughout the United States, and the vision comes to life right here in Little Rock. Heifer Village is their hands-on educational facility that offers interactive exhibits to details the organization's mission and worldwide efforts.

1 World Ave., Little Rock
501-907-2697, heifer.org

TIP
Heifer International is located in downtown Little Rock's newest neighborhood: East Village. Check out the various bars and restaurants nearby.

BE INSPIRED
AT THE ARKANSAS LITERARY FESTIVAL

Each year the Central Arkansas Library System celebrates authors, screenwriters, and artists from all over the world. With over eighty presenters in the lineup, there's something for everyone. You can catch a Pulitzer Prize-winning poet, notable journalist, or even your favorite sports reporter, up close and personal. Adults don't want to miss Author! Author! the opening reception where you can not only get your book signed, but also snap a selfie. Then you can move about town to the varied panels and sessions and be inspired. There is always a special event for children. Many are held at the Hillary Rodham Clinton Children's Library and feature child stars in the industry or those who are specifically working in the genre.

arkansasliteraryfestival.org

BUY A BOOK OR PIECE OF ART
AT PYRAMID ART, BOOKS, AND CUSTOM FRAMING AND HEARNE FINE ART

Here's an idea: bring in your old books to donate to the free book display, then buy a new one! Opened in 1988, this institution is known for its African American literature. With many bookstores of its kind closed due to the recession, Pyramid still stands. When you are done browsing the book section, take in the latest art display. Right next door is Hearne Fine Art Gallery, which houses some of the most profound exhibitions—art lovers, you will not be disappointed! Owners Archie and Garbo Hearne view their space as more than a place to shop, but also as a source of culture and community enrichment. Their commitment to the preservation and promotion of African American fine art and literature is an experience you don't want to miss!

1001 Wright Ave., Little Rock
501-372-5824
pyramidbks.net

GET IN TOUCH WITH NATURE
AT THE CENTRAL ARKANSAS NATURE CENTER

Arkansas is The Natural State, so a visit to Little Rock wouldn't be complete without a little outdoor activity or education. The Witt Stephens Jr. Central Arkansas Nature Center is just the place to go. We know the name is really long but it's a fun place to see a variety of animals and native plants and participate in watchable wildlife activities. They even have aquariums that showcase our state's fish. The facility is located in Riverfront Park and overlooks the Arkansas River. Exhibits highlight the role of fish and wildlife management and many of the projects conducted throughout the history of the Arkansas Game and Fish Commission. Best news, admission to the nature center is free!

602 President Clinton Ave., Little Rock
501-907-0636
agfc.com

SUBMERGE IN HISTORY
AT THE ARKANSAS INLAND
MARITIME MUSEUM

Veterans of World War II told stories of the USS *Razorback* for years after the war. Those who lived aboard the longest-serving submarine in the world were proud of the five combat patrols and many successes of the submarine and its crew. Now, that very same submarine has found a home in North Little Rock at the Arkansas Inland Maritime Museum. Take a tour or have a sleepover. The submarine has functioning heating and air-conditioning and friendly staff available to help you do it all. Before you go down under, be sure to check out the tugboat USS *Hoga* (YT-146). The *Hoga* is the last floating vessel that served in Pearl Harbor during the Japanese attack on December 7, 1941. The Arkansas Inland Museum is the only museum, outside of Honolulu, Hawaii, to display two naval vessels that bookend World War II. It is certainly the place to go for a glimpse of US naval history.

120 Riverfront Park Dr., North Little Rock
501-371-8320
AIMMuseum.org

CELEBRATE ARKANSAS'S AFRICAN AMERICAN HISTORY
AT MOSAIC TEMPLARS CULTURAL CENTER

The story of African American Arkansans is celebrated at Mosaic Templars Cultural Center. Here you can view permanent exhibits that tell both the past and living history of African Americans in Arkansas from 1870 to present. Learn about post-Civil War life which brought about a boom in black entrepreneurship along West Ninth Street, the story behind the Mosaic Templars of America building and organization, and finally, the living history of the Arkansas Black Hall of Fame. Many well-known temporary exhibits have also made a stop in Little Rock, including Shades of Greatness: Art Inspired by Negro Leagues Baseball, The Fine Art of Jazz, and the Inauguration of Hope, a life size memorial to the historic inauguration of President Barak Obama.

501 W. 9th St., Little Rock
501-683-3593
mosaictemplarscenter.com

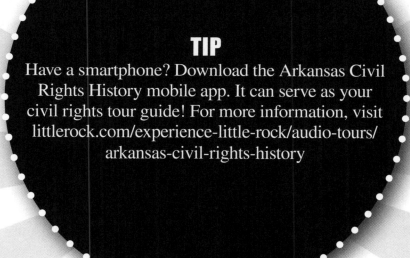

TIP

Have a smartphone? Download the Arkansas Civil Rights History mobile app. It can serve as your civil rights tour guide! For more information, visit littlerock.com/experience-little-rock/audio-tours/ arkansas-civil-rights-history

EXPLORE ARKANSAS'S COLORFUL STATEHOOD
AT THE OLD STATEHOUSE MUSEUM

Another one of Arkansas's National Historic Landmarks, the Old State House Museum, is as old as the state itself. Built in 1833, the original building served as the state capitol before becoming a museum in 1947. The museum is home to Arkansas artifacts that help preserve and tell the story of our history. The collections include a quilt exhibit, pottery collection, sports artifacts, Civil War collection, women's history collection, and many more. Two of the most fascinating are the collections of gowns worn by first ladies to government inaugurations and collections from the first families. Here you can find Hillary Clinton's inaugural gown, the typewriter of Governor John Little, and the wallet of Governor Orval Faubus. You can take a guided tour through the museum or go on your own.

300 Markham St., Little Rock
501-324-9685
oldstatehouse.com

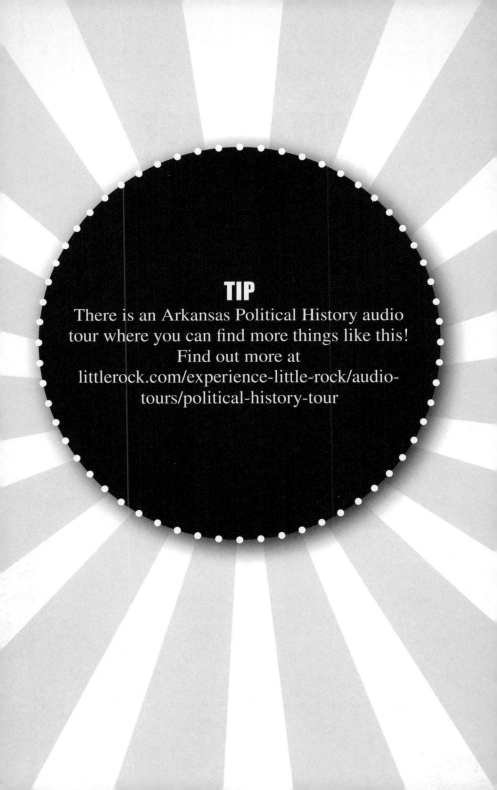

TIP

There is an Arkansas Political History audio tour where you can find more things like this! Find out more at littlerock.com/experience-little-rock/audio-tours/political-history-tour

PAY HOMAGE TO OUR HEROES
AT MACARTHUR MUSEUM OF ARKANSAS MILITARY HISTORY

Arkansas is working hard to preserve important history for future generations. To learn about General Douglas MacArthur, whose outstanding military career includes a Congressional Medal of Honor, citizens can visit the MacArthur Museum of Arkansas Military History. Located inside a National Historic Landmark, the Arsenal Building, this museum features exhibits dedicated to Arkansas's role in the Civil War. Here you can also find a stained glass window dedicated to David O. Dodd, the Little Rock boy who was hanged as a Confederate spy. Although history of the Confederacy is somewhat controversial in modern day, it still stands as a part of our past. Many lost their lives. You can learn more about their stories and the stories of all of Arkansas's proud military personnel at the MacArthur Museum of Arkansas Military History.

503 E. 9th St., Little Rock
501-376-4602
macarthurparklr.com

● ●

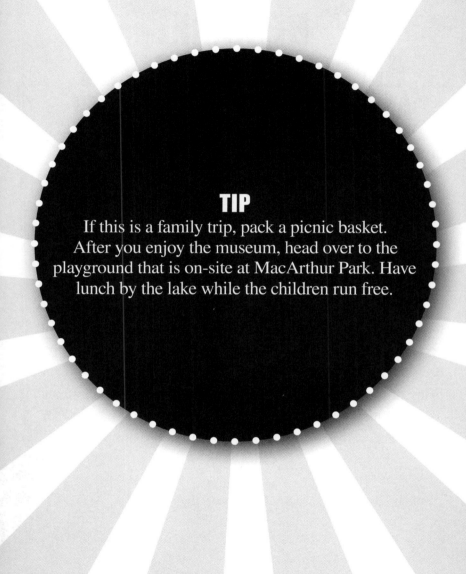

TIP

If this is a family trip, pack a picnic basket. After you enjoy the museum, head over to the playground that is on-site at MacArthur Park. Have lunch by the lake while the children run free.

BECOME AN ART ENTHUSIAST
AT THE ARKANSAS ARTS CENTER

In 1959 what was once just a vision of the members of the Fine Arts Club of Arkansas came to life in a big way. The Arkansas Arts Center was born, adding an educational venue for those who loved the arts or simply wanted to know more. The permanent collection includes numerous renowned drawings, contemporary crafts, paintings, photographs, and prints. Today, the vision has grown, and so has its influence on the local community. They offer a variety of classes for the local community, as well as productions through their Children's Theatre. Here students have a place to perfect their talents outside of school. The Children's Theatre has been recognized as one of the best in the region and performs many of the classics. As another way to show their commitment to the community, the Children's Theatre has "pay what you can" nights. This way no one is denied a chance to experience art.

9th and Commerce, Little Rock
501-372-4000
arkansasartscenter.org

TRAVERSE THE ARKANSAS RIVER
AT ROCK TOWN RIVER OUTFITTERS

This kayak and paddleboard rental business is located on the north banks of the Arkansas River at Rockwater Marina. Complete with guided river tours, Rock Town River Outfitters provides a wonderful opportunity to experience greater Little Rock's natural scenic beauty and outdoor water recreation. They also operate a bike rental shop in Little Rock's River Market District. You can explore on your own, or plan to join one of their guided tours. They offer a variety of guided tours covering everything from history to beer! If you travel with your own bike, they also offer full service for repairs and tune-ups.

1600 Rockwater Blvd., North Little Rock
400 President Clinton Ave., Little Rock
501-690-2277
rocktownriveroutfitters.com

SEE HISTORY UP CLOSE
AT THE DAISY BATES HOUSE

Daisy Bates was an American civil rights legend. Once the owner of the *Arkansas State Press*, a statewide newspaper with a focus on African American issues, Bates would go down in history books as the president of the Arkansas chapter of the NAACP who served as the advisor and mentor to the Little Rock Nine. Meetings happened at her home, which still stands today on Little Rock's Westside. It was declared a National Historic Landmark in 2001 and has been restored as closely as possible to her original décor. The most striking thing about the home is the huge bay window. During a time when hate crimes often resulted in bricks being thrown, the window symbolizes Daisy Bates's strength and courage. See history, up close and personal, at the Daisy Bates House. Be sure to call for a private tour. The house is not open to the public.

1207 W. 28th St., Little Rock
501-374-1957
nps.gov/nr/travel/civilrights/ar2.htm

REMINISCE
AT THE ESSE PURSE MUSEUM

While many women have a distinct purse collection, there are very few museums dedicated to the handbag. Amsterdam, Seoul, and Little Rock are the only three places in the world with a physical museum. The permanent exhibit traces the evolution of the 20th century American woman through the purses and contents within. Many temporary exhibits including Barbie: The Vintage Years and Handbag for Hillary also travel through. In case you are inspired to pick up something new, Esse also has a store featuring original designs in purses, jewelry, and accessories. Visit their website. Many of the unique designs are available online.

1510 S. Main St., Little Rock
501-916-9022
essepursemuseum.com

TAKE A CHILD
TO THE HILLARY RODHAM CLINTON CHILDREN'S LIBRARY

Before she was First Lady of the United States, Hillary Rodham Clinton was Arkansas's First Lady and the Clinton influence on the capital city is evident everywhere you turn. The Clinton Presidential Library helped revive the downtown, and the airport bears both Bill's and Hillary's names, but as a lover of books, we could not be more proud of the Hillary Rodham Clinton Children's Library. Actually it's much more than a library. This is the place where young minds go to grow. They offer many activities and programs for students of all ages. For homework needs, you will find a computer lab and laptops available for check out. Take a child to the children's library where they can witness a building designed just for them.

4800 W. 10th St., Little Rock
501-978-3870
cals.org/childrens-library

Looking for great restaurants that the kids will love? Try these:

All Aboard Restaurant & Grill
all-aboardrestaurant.com

Purple Cow
purplecowlr.com

Dave & Buster's
daveandbusters.com

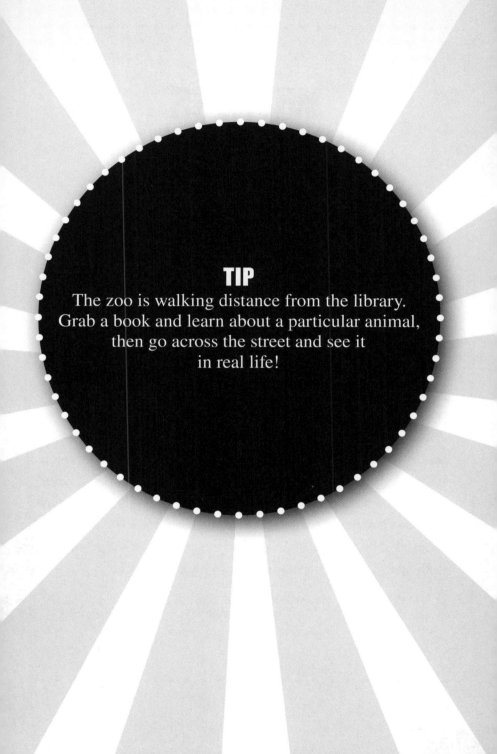

TIP

The zoo is walking distance from the library.
Grab a book and learn about a particular animal,
then go across the street and see it
in real life!

WITNESS ARCHITECTURAL EXCELLENCE
AT THE ARKANSAS STATE CAPITOL

Constructed between 1899 and 1915 for $2.3 million, the Arkansas State Capitol is a sight to see. No short description will do it justice. Designed by architects George Mann and Cass Gilbert, the neoclassical style of the building holds true to the twentieth century, featuring six bronze doors and three chandeliers crafted by Tiffany's of New York. Although the building itself is quite impressive, the grounds of the Arkansas State Capitol have several monuments that are certainly worth a visit. You can visit the only civil rights memorial located on any state capitol grounds in the south, *Testament*, which honors the Little Rock Nine. The Vietnam Veterans Memorial is a smaller version of the memorial in our nation's capital. With over six hundred names inscribed on the black marble wall designed by Stephen Gartmann, the memorial was dedicated in 1987 and is also believed to be the first of its kind on the grounds of a state capitol. Both memorials are popular stops for visitors and locals.

500 Woodlane Ave., Little Rock
501-682-5080
sos.arkansas.gov/state-capitol

GO BACK IN TIME
AT THE ARKANSAS KOREAN WAR VETERANS MEMORIAL

Much like the Vietnam Veterans Memorial, Little Rock pays homage to those who lost their lives in the Korean War. Located in the historic MacArthur Park, over four hundred names are listed on black granite panels. The majority of funding for this memorial came from the Republic of Korea, which makes it very unique. Legend says that the country wanted to pay homage to those who helped them gain their freedom. Included in the memorial are seven-foot statues of soldiers and Korean children. This reminds us all of the sacrifice made by military personnel. The Arkansas Korean War Veterans Memorial is said to be one of the most impressive in the United States.

503 E. 9th St., Little Rock
501-376-4602
macarthurparklr.com

TIP
There are more monuments displayed on the grounds of the Arkansas State Capitol.

LEARN ABOUT TAEKWONDO
AT H.U. LEE INTERNATIONAL GATE AND GARDEN

Little Rock has a unique relationship with taekwondo. Each year thousands flood the streets from all over the world to attend the ATA International World Expo. What many do not realize is that the international headquarters for this association is located right here in Little Rock. The H.U. Lee International Gate and Garden honors the founder of ATA, Eternal Grand Master Haeng Ung Lee. Before transitioning in 2000, Grand Master Lee dedicated his life to sharing the art of taekwondo. The garden pays tribute to his legacy and also serves as a salute to friendship between South Korea and America. The gate which graces the front of the garden was handcrafted by South Korean artisans, and is located in downtown, adjacent to the Statehouse Convention Center.

7 Statehouse Plaza, Little Rock, 501-376-4781
grandmasterhulee.com/gate-and-garden

TIP
If you want to learn more about ATA International check out their World Headquarters, complete with exhibits and history about their organization. 1800 Riverfront Dr., Little Rock, 501-568-2821
ataonline.com

GET GONE WITH THE WIND
AT THE OLD MILL

In the opening credits of the famous motion picture *Gone with the Wind*, you can see the Old Mill. This landmark located in North Little Rock has been made famous by its appearance in the film and attracts visitors from all over the world. Completed in 1933, the mill was the brainchild of Justin Matthews. Matthews wanted to recreate an old water-powered grist mill from the 1880s for a park area in his new housing development. Today the mill is a city park and the landscaping is cared for by the Master Gardeners of Little Rock. Many use the park as a backdrop for family photos. The Old Mill is said to be the only remaining structure from the classic film.

Fairway Ave. and Lakeshore Dr., North Little Rock
501-791-8537

TOUR OLD VICTORIAN-STYLE HOMES
IN THE QUAPAW QUARTER

Little Rock has something special for architecture and history lovers alike. Almost ten square miles of restored historic homes make up the Quapaw Quarter. Although Victorian style is my personal favorite, in one block you can view five different types of architecture. The Queen Anne style featuring wraparound porches, classic columns, and huge bay windows is very popular. In an effort to foster appreciation for historic buildings, owners have opened their homes for a spring tour once a year since 1963. Many visitors are so enamored by the district that they decide to become residents. When this happens, they are certainly in good company, as the Arkansas Governor's Mansion is also in the area. The district is managed by the Quapaw Quarter Association. Visit their website for springtime tour dates.

615 E. Capitol Ave., Little Rock
501-371-0075
quapaw.com

TIP

Look for the Villa Marre, now a private residence. It was the Sugarbaker Design Studio from the television show *Designing Women*. Also, if you are looking for some fun, try Little Rock's escape rooms, both are in the Quapaw Quarter!

Mystery Mansion
2122 S. Broadway, Little Rock
501-580-1325
mysterymansionescape.com

The Escape Little Rock
1214 S. Main St., Little Rock
501-379-9908
theescapelittlerock.com

RIDE
THE ROCK REGION METRO STREETCAR

Downtown Little Rock and North Little Rock feature replicas of vintage trolleys that give patrons not only a unique way to travel, but also a great way to tour the cities. They connect the twin cities through a 3.4-mile streetcar system that makes it easy to move between attractions. Those being served include the Verizon Arena, the Statehouse Convention Center, multiple museums, and several hotels and restaurants downtown. The drivers give you an overview of attractions as you ride. The best thing about the trolley is that it's inexpensive. With rides costing $1 each way, it's a fun activity to do with the entire family.

901 N. Maple St., Little Rock
501-375-6717
rrmetro.org/services/streetcar

PARTY WITH THE PENGUINS
AT THE LITTLE ROCK ZOO

With over seven hundred animals at the Little Rock Zoo, we find the penguins most impressive. Maybe we're biased, but there is just something unique about seeing South African penguins in Little Rock. The Penguin Pointe exhibit opened in March of 2011 and has been a crowd favorite since the beginning. The exhibit boasts a realistic setting for the warmer-climate species of penguins and is the largest the Little Rock Zoo has ever done. Often times you have to drag children away from Penguin Pointe as they too are fascinated by the animal. The exhibit is also home to many private parties. The Little Rock Zoo offers on-site catering for your special event. Now we're not saying that the elephants, cheetahs, and reptiles are not interesting to see, but we are saying, don't leave the zoo before you party with the penguins.

1 Zoo Dr., Little Rock
501-666-2406
littlerockzoo.com

TIP
During Halloween Boo-at-the-Zoo is one of the zoo's most popular events. The adult night is where grownups go to be a kid again.

SHOPPING AND FASHION

EXPLORE
PARK PLAZA MALL

For a long time, residents of Little Rock went to Park Plaza for all their shopping needs. This midtown mall has been a staple in the community for as long as we can remember. Anchored between the men's and women's divisions of Dillard's department store, here you can find many popular brands such as H&M, Banana Republic, Express, and Eddie Bauer. The food court features Chick-fil-A, the local flavor of David's Burgers, and several others. Little Rock is home to Dillard's department store's corporate headquarters, so it comes as no surprise that the shopping haven serves as the mall's only major department store; however, Dillard's has it all. From apparel to housewares, this retail giant serves Little Rock well.

6000 W. Markham St., Little Rock
501-664-4956
parkplazamall.com

SHOP
AT THE PROMENADE

This outdoor mall in west Little Rock has quickly become very popular. It features twelve restaurants, including Local Lime, BRAVO! Cucina Italiana, and Ya Ya's Euro Bistro. The Promenade is the mall to visit if you want to shop, eat, drink, and see a movie all in the same place. The Chenal 9 IMAX has the city's only IMAX screen running feature films. The Promenade is also where you will find Little Rock's only Apple Store. Enjoy specialty shops like Just Dogs! Gourmet, which specializes in all-natural treats for our four-legged family members; and Belle & Blush, a high-end luxury boutique offering cosmetics, accessories, and a host of other must-haves. Visit the website for a complete directory and be sure to browse Anthropologie; the brand is known for its quality and the store happens to be one of my favorite places to shop.

17711 Chenal Pkwy. Ste. I-114, Little Rock
501-821-5552
chenalshopping.com

TIP
Want more outdoor shopping? Try Shackleford Crossing or Pleasant Ridge Town Center.

FIND A DEAL
AT THE OUTLETS OF LITTLE ROCK

In fall of 2015, three hundred twenty-five thousand square feet of shopping opened in Arkansas's capital city. The Outlets have brought over one thousand jobs to the city and are contributing handsomely to Little Rock's tax collections. Needless to say, so far they have been a welcomed addition. Aside from the retail outlets like Gap, J. Crew, and Old Navy, there is also a Beef Jerky Outlet with more than seventy types of the dried meat, including ostrich. It is not uncommon to find sales promotions at the Outlets of Little Rock; you can view in-store events on the website. Located at Interstates 30 and 430, you could easily turn this shopping experience into a family affair. There are also numerous restaurants and entertainment offerings in the surrounding Gateway Town Center, including Arkansas's only Movie Tavern, Bass Pro Shops and Dave & Buster's.

11201 Bass Pro Pkwy., Little Rock
501-455-9100
outletsoflittlerock.com

EXPLORE LOCAL BOUTIQUES
IN THE HEIGHTS

Tired of run-of-the-mill shopping? The Heights in Little Rock is the place for you. This charming neighborhood, considered one of the most affluent in Little Rock, offers plenty of upscale retail stores and boutiques. Mostly locally owned and operated, with a few national chains, there is something in The Heights for every shopper. From clothing and accessories to cosmetics and gourmet foods, this eclectic neighborhood is the perfect place for retail therapy. Here you will find Bella Boutique, a fun trendy gift shop; Terry's Finer Foods, a gourmet food market featuring fresh meat and seafood; and a host of other unique options. Sure, everyone likes a traditional shopping mall, but the shops and boutiques in The Heights offer a shopping experience that is off the beaten path. For a list of stores and shops, visit The Heights Neighborhood Association webpage.

intheheightslr.com

TIP
The Heights also offers a great selection of restaurants. ZAZA's and Cafe Prego, which are both mentioned in this book, are in The Heights.

SHOP AND SIP
IN HILLCREST

Although the two are very close, Hillcrest and The Heights are two distinctly different neighborhoods. Hillcrest is a National Register of Historic Places location because it is one of the oldest residential districts in the city. Many of the locations mentioned in this book, including Bossa Nova, Ciao Baci, and Kemuri are in Hillcrest. The first Thursday of every month, shops and restaurants offer discounts, later hours, and live music. There is lots of sidewalk traffic during Sip and Shop, some for the drinks, but mostly for the shops. In Hillcrest you can find Hillcrest Designer Jewelry, an upscale diamond wholesaler, and Box Turtle, a colorful shopping boutique. For a list of merchants, visit the Hillcrest Merchants Association page. You will be glad you did!

hillcrestmerchants.net

PICK UP A SOUVENIR
AT SHOP THE ROCK

You can't leave the city without an official Little Rock souvenir. If you are a local who wants to show your Little Rock pride or a visitor who wants to take home a piece of the magic, Shop the Rock in the River Market is the place for you. They have apparel, books, locally-labeled items, and glassware. You can even find Wicked Mix, Arkansas's own trail mix that will have you salivating for more! Trust me, try the Wicked Mix White Chocolate. It is a winning combination of original, smoky chipotle, and white chocolate. It will make you cheat on any diet! Just in case you have willpower that we don't, Shop the Rock also carries Ferneau seasonings, Van's honey, and Redneck Gourmet items, all locally-labeled right here in Central Arkansas.

400 President Clinton Ave., Little Rock
501-320-3515
shoptherock.biz

TIP
The River Market District has several great local shops for retail therapy!
rivermarket.info/shop

BE NATURAL
AT THE FARMERS MARKET

Each May through September the Little Rock Farmers Market is open in downtown. Since 1974, the market, like those in many other cities, has been the go-to venue for fresh fruits and vegetables. But, why stop there? The Farmers Market in Little Rock features a wide variety of vendors. From locally prepared foods to arts and crafts, it has become a popular Saturday stop for many. Another unique thing about the Farmers Market in Little Rock is that rain or shine, the show goes on! Because it is held in open air pavilions, you don't have to worry about getting wet. For a full list of vendors visit the website below.

400 President Clinton Ave., Little Rock
501-375-2552
rivermarket.info/learn-more/farmers-market

TIP
The SoMa (South Main) neighborhood also hosts a great Farmers Market. Theirs is on Sundays in the Bernice Garden.
somalittlerock.com

PURCHASE
A TOP-OF-THE-LINE BICYCLE AT ORBEA USA OR ALLIED CYCLE WORKS

What began as a handgun venture in the city of Eibar in Spain between three brothers evolved into upscale bicycles by 1930. Thanks to Tour De France champion Mariano Cañardo, Orbea gained recognition as a cycling brand. By 1980 the brand was prevalent on the competitive cycling scene and toward the end of the decade had ventured into mountain bikes. Today North Little Rock is home to the Spanish bicycle manufacturer's North American headquarters. If you are looking for a top-of-the-line bicycle or just want to explore what Orbea has to offer, stop in and check out their inventory. New to the elite cycle scene is Allied Cycle Works, based right here in Little Rock. Allied is a premium American bicycle brand that engineers and manufactures its own products in the USA. Their carbon fiber bicycles can be completely customized to your specifications, allowing you to select the color, treatment and components you desire.

Orbea USA
700 W. Broadway, North Little Rock
501-280-9700, orbea.com

Allied Cycle Works
2201 Brookwood Dr. Ste. 108, Little Rock
844-442-8356, alliedcycleworks.com

Photo provided courtesy of
Little Rock Convention & Visitors Bureau.

SUGGESTED
ITINERARIES

PROGRESSIVE DINNER PARTY

Drink Like a Local with Locally Labeled, 2

Eat Like a President at Doe's Eat Place, 5

Gratify Your Sweet Tooth at Loblolly Creamery, 18

A ROMANTIC WEEKEND

Sip Grand High Tea at Empress of Little Rock, 63

Dine at 42 Bar and Table, 30

Stroll the Junction Bridge Pedestrian Walkway, 77

Create Your Own "Wish You Were Here" Postcard, 78

Laugh at the Loony Bin Comedy Club, 46

Light Up the Night With River Lights in the Rock, 48

Catch a Performance at the Robinson Performance Hall, 47

WHERE THE SPORTS PEOPLE GO

Drink Like a Local with Locally Labeled, 2

Play at Dave & Buster's, 29

Find Your Favorite Beer at Flying Saucer, 60

FOR THE OUTDOORS TYPE

CIVIL RIGHTS TOUR

FAMILY FUN

PARTY ALL NIGHT LONG

FOR THE MUSIC LOVERS

AWESOME DIVES

UPSCALE VENUES

ENVIRONMENTALISTS HAVENS

Photo provided courtesy of
Little Rock Convention & Visitors Bureau.

ACTIVITIES
BY SEASON

WINTER

Paint with a Twist at Painting with a Twist, 57

Sip Grand High Tea at Empress of Little Rock, 63

Reserve a Lane at Dust Bowl Lanes & Lounge, 67

Shoot Hoops with the Little Rock Trojans at UA Little Rock, 69

Get High at Altitude Trampoline Park or Third Realm Extreme
  Air Sports, 80

Skate at Arkansas Skatium, 81

Do It Yourself at The Painted Pig, 83

Conduct an Experiment at the Museum of Discovery, 89

Discover History at the Little Rock Central High School National Historic
  Site, 90

Explore Park Plaza Mall, 120

SPRING

Catch a Performance at the Robinson Performance Hall, 47

Eat Greek at the International Greek Food Festival, 50

Catch a Movie in the Park, 54

Cheer on the Arkansas Travelers, 68

Climb Pinnacle Mountain, 76

Get Gone with the Wind at the Old Mill, 113

Shop and Sip in Hillcrest, 124

Tour Old Victorian-Style Homes in the Quapaw Quarter, 114

INDEX